REPORTING INTELLECTUAL PROPERTY CRIME:

A Guide for Victims of Copyright Infringement, Trademark Counterfeiting, and Trade Secret Theft

Table of Contents

What Are Copyrights, Trademarks, and Trade Secrets?

The United States has created enforceable rights in "intangibles" that are known as intellectual property, including copyrights, trademarks, and trade secrets. ***Copyright law*** provides federal protection against infringement of certain exclusive rights, such as reproduction and distribution, of "original works of authorship," including computer software, literary works, musical works, and motion pictures. 17 U.S.C. §§ 102(a), 106. The use of a commercial brand to identify a product is protected by ***trademark law***, which prohibits the unauthorized use of "any word, name, symbol, or device" used by a person "to identify and distinguish his or her goods, including a unique product, from those manufactured or sold by others and to indicate the source of the goods." 15 U.S.C. § 1127. Finally, ***trade secret law*** prohibits the unauthorized disclosure of any confidential and proprietary business information, such as a formula, device, or compilation of information but only when that information possesses an independent economic value because it is secret and the owner has taken reasonable measures to keep it secret. For more information on these rights and how they are criminally enforced, see Prosecuting Intellectual Property Crimes (4th ed. 2013), U.S. Department of Justice, Computer Crime and Intellectual Property Section (forthcoming *http://www.cybercrime.gov*).

How Can Intellectual Property Be Stolen?

Intellectual property can be stolen (*i.e.*, infringed or misappropriated) in many ways. For example, copyrighted works, such as movies, music, books, business software or games, may be illegally infringed by reproducing or distributing unauthorized copies of such works either online or by manufacturing and distributing infringing CDs or DVDs containing the unauthorized content. A trademark may be infringed by selling goods, labels or other packaging containing a counterfeit mark. A highly protected trade secret can be surreptitiously misappropriated from its owner either by a company insider or by someone outside a company and used to benefit a competitor.

When Is an Intellectual Property Violation a Federal Crime?

Although individuals or companies can pursue civil remedies to address violations of their intellectual property rights, criminal sanctions are often warranted to ensure sufficient punishment and deterrence of wrongful activity. Congress has continually expanded and strengthened criminal laws for violations of intellectual property rights to protect innovation, to keep pace with evolving technology and, significantly, to ensure that egregious or persistent intellectual property violations do not merely become a standard cost of doing business for defendants. Among the most significant provisions are the following:

❑ **Counterfeit Trademarks:** The Trademark Counterfeiting Act, 18 U.S.C. § 2320(b)(1)(A), provides penalties of up to ten years' imprisonment and a $2 million fine for a defendant who intentionally "traffics in goods or services and knowingly uses a counterfeit mark on or in connection with such goods or services," or intentionally "traffics in labels, . . . documentation, or packaging . . . knowing that a counterfeit mark has been applied thereto." Section 2320(b)(3) provides penalties of up to twenty years' imprisonment and a $5 million fine for a defendant who intentionally traffics in counterfeit drugs or certain counterfeit military goods or services.

❑ **Counterfeit Labeling:** The counterfeit labeling provisions of 18 U.S.C. § 2318 prohibit trafficking in counterfeit labels designed to be affixed to movies, music, software, and literary, pictorial, graphic, or sculptural works and works of visual art as well as trafficking in counterfeit documentation or packaging for such works. Violations are punishable by up to five years' imprisonment and a $250,000 fine.

❑ **Criminal Copyright Infringement:** Copyright infringement is a felony punishable by up to three years' imprisonment and a $250,000 fine under 17 U.S.C. § 506(a) and 18 U.S.C. § 2319 where a defendant willfully *reproduces* or *distributes* at least ten copies of one or more copyrighted works with a total retail value of more than $2,500 within a 180-day period. The maximum penalty rises to five years' imprisonment if the defendant also acted "for purposes of commercial advantage or private financial gain." Misdemeanor copyright infringement occurs where the value exceeds $1,000 or where the defendant willfully violated any of the exclusive rights "for purposes of commercial advantage or private financial gain."

❑ **Pre-Release Criminal Copyright Infringement:** Pre-release piracy, *i.e.*, willful infringement "by the distribution of a work being prepared for commercial distribution, by making it available on a computer network accessible to members of the public, if such person knew or should have known that the work was intended for commercial distribution," is a felony punishable by up to three years' imprisonment and a $250,000 fine under 17 U.S.C. § 506(a)(1)(C) and 18 U.S.C. § 2319(d). The maximum penalty rises to five years' imprisonment if the defendant also acted "for purposes of commercial advantage or private financial gain."

❑ **Theft of Trade Secrets:** The Economic Espionage Act contains two separate provisions that criminalize the theft of trade secrets. The first provision, 18 U.S.C. § 1831, prohibits the theft of trade secrets for the benefit of a foreign government, instrumentality, or agent, and is punishable by up to 15 years' imprisonment and a $5,000,000 fine. The second, 18 U.S.C. § 1832, prohibits the commercial theft of trade secrets to benefit someone other than the owner, and is punishable by up to ten years' imprisonment and a $250,000 fine. The penalties are higher for defendants who are companies. The statute broadly defines the term "trade secret" to include all types of information that the owner has taken reasonable measures to keep secret and that itself has independent economic value. 18 U.S.C. § 1839(3). Federal law also provides special protections to victims in trade secret cases to ensure that the confidentiality of trade secret information is preserved during the course of criminal proceedings. Specifically, the statute expressly states that courts "shall enter such orders and take such action as may be necessary and appropriate to preserve the confidentiality of trade secrets, consistent with the requirements of the Federal Rules of Criminal and Civil Procedure, the Federal Rules of Evidence, and all other applicable laws." 18 U.S.C. § 1835.

❑ **Camcording:** The Family Entertainment and Copyright Act criminalizes the use of camcorders and similar devices to record movies playing in public theaters. "Camcording" is a felony punishable by up to three years imprisonment' and a $250,000 fine under 18 U.S.C. §2319B(a) where a defendant "knowingly uses or attempts to use an audiovisual recording device to transmit or make a copy of a motion picture. . . in a motion picture exhibition facility."

Why Should You Report Intellectual Property Crime?

Intellectual property is an increasingly important part of the United States' economy, representing its fastest growing sector, contributing billions of dollars to America's gross domestic product, and employing over 55 million Americans, according to the Global Intellectual Property Center. (*http://www.theglobalipcenter.com/pages/why-are-intellectual-property-rights-important*). As the nation continues to shift from an industrial economy to an information-based economy, the assets of the country are increasingly based in intellectual property. In addition, intellectual property crime in the United States and abroad not only threatens our nation's economic well-being, it can also place at risk the public health and safety of our citizens and our national security.

In recognition of this trend, the Department of Justice is waging an aggressive campaign against intellectual property crime in all its forms. In 2010, the Attorney General established a Task Force on Intellectual Property ("IPTF") as part of a Department-wide initiative to confront the growing number of domestic and international IP crimes. Chaired by the Deputy Attorney General, the IPTF brings high level attention and coordination to the Department's efforts to combat intellectual property crime. Through the IPTF's support and guidance, the Department has continued to prioritize criminal intellectual property investigations and prosecutions nationwide and has increased both the prosecutorial and investigative resources brought to bear on the growing problem of intellectual property theft. For more information on the Department's efforts see the IPTF website at *http://www.justice.gov/dag/iptaskforce/*, as well as the Department's Annual PRO IP Act Reports from fiscal years 2009 through 2012. See *http://www.justice.gov/criminal/cybercrime/documents.html*.

Effective prosecution of intellectual property crime, however, also requires substantial assistance from its victims. Because the victims of intellectual property crime are often in the best position to detect a theft, law enforcement authorities cannot act in many cases unless the crimes are reported in the first place. Once these crimes are reported, federal law enforcement authorities need to quickly identify the facts that establish jurisdiction for the potential intellectual property offenses, such as federal copyright and trademark registration information, as well as facts concerning the extent of a victim's potential loss, the nature of the theft, and possible suspects. In a digital world where evidence can disappear at the click of a mouse, swift investigation is often essential to successful intellectual property prosecutions.

Accordingly, the Department of Justice has created this guide for victims to facilitate the flow of critical information from victims of intellectual property crimes to law enforcement authorities. The Department of Justice's goal is to make it as easy as possible to report incidents of intellectual property crime to law enforcement authorities, including whom to contact and what to tell them.

> **Note**: The guidelines set forth below seek information that, in the experience of Department of Justice prosecutors and investigators, is useful or even critical to the successful prosecution of the most common intellectual property crimes. These guidelines are not intended to be exhaustive, nor does the presence or absence of responsive information from the victim necessarily determine the outcome of an investigation.

What Should You Do If You Are Victimized?

Victims of intellectual property crime, such as copyright infringement, trademark counterfeiting, and theft of trade secrets, often conduct internal investigations before referring matters to law enforcement. These investigations can encompass a variety of steps, including interviewing witnesses, acquiring samples of the counterfeit goods, conducting surveillance of suspects, and examining computers and other evidence. Victims can maximize the benefit of these independent investigative activities as follows:

❑ **Document All Investigative Steps:** To avoid duplication of effort and retracing of steps, internal investigations should seek to create a record of all investigative steps that can later be presented to law enforcement, if necessary. If a victim company observes counterfeit goods for sale online and makes a purchase, for example, investigators should record the domain name, URL, and IP address of the website, the date and time of the purchase, the method of payment, and the date and manner of delivery of the goods. Any subsequent examination or testing of the goods should then be recorded in a document that identifies the telltale characteristics of theft or specific indicators of counterfeiting, such as lack of a security seal, poor quality, failure to meet specifications, packaging, or the like.

Similarly, in the case of a suspected theft of trade secrets, any internal investigation or surveillance of the suspect, or a competitor believed to be using the stolen information, should be recorded. A record of any interviews with suspects or witnesses should be made by tape or in writing. The pertinent confidentiality agreements, security policies, and access logs should also be gathered and maintained to facilitate review and reduce the risk of deletion or destruction.

❑ **Preserve the Evidence:** Any physical, documentary, or digital evidence acquired in the course of an internal investigation should be preserved for later use in a legal proceeding. In the online theft example identified above, victims should print out or obtain a digital copy of the offending website, preserve any e-mails or texts related to the counterfeit item(s), and safely store any infringing goods and their packaging, which may contain details of their origin. Additionally, print out and preserve any documentation of the course of dealing with the offending seller, including (but not limited to) any sales agreements or contracts, communications about the purchase, or other such documentation. If the computer of an employee suspected of stealing trade secrets has been seized, any forensic analysis should be performed on a copy of the data, or "digital image," to undermine claims that the evidence has been altered or corrupted.

❑ **Contact Law Enforcement Right Away:** Victims can maximize their legal remedies for intellectual property crime by making contact with law enforcement soon after its detection. Early referral to law enforcement is the best way to ensure that evidence of an intellectual property crime is properly secured and that all investigative avenues are fully explored, such as the execution of search warrants and possible undercover law enforcement activities. Communication with law enforcement authorities at the onset of suspected violations also allows a victim to coordinate administrative or civil proceedings with possible criminal enforcement. Use the reporting checklists set forth later in this guide to organize the information you gather and provide the necessary information to your law enforcement contact.

Where Do I Report an Intellectual Property Crime?

Although there are a variety of ways to report an intellectual property crime to law enforcement, the following list identifies the most common and efficient investigative and prosecutorial contacts.

Federal Investigative Contacts

❑ **National Intellectual Property Rights Coordination Center ("IPR Center").** The IPR Center is an interagency task force led by U.S. Immigration and Customs Enforcement, Homeland Security Investigations ("ICE-HSI"). The IPR Center is a collaborative effort by over 19 U.S. government investigative and regulatory agency partners, including the Federal Bureau of Investigation ("FBI"), as well as representatives from Canada and Mexico, that work together to combat intellectual property crime. IPR Center partners work together to investigate and deconflict case leads, interdict counterfeit and pirated goods at the borders, and provide extensive training and outreach. The IPR Center also works closely with the Department of Justice through the Criminal Division's Computer Crime and Intellectual Property Section. The IPR Center encourages victims to visit its website at *http://www.IPRCenter.gov* to obtain more information about the IPR Center and to report violations of intellectual property rights online or by emailing *IPRCenter@dhs.gov*.

❑ **Federal Bureau of Investigation ("FBI").** The FBI's Criminal Investigative Division includes an Intellectual Property Rights Unit ("IPR Unit") that oversees its national intellectual property program, which includes dedicated FBI Special Agents who are responsible for the investigation and prosecution of intellectual property crime. The FBI's IPR Unit is headquartered at the IPR Center and the FBI Special Agents dedicated to investigating IP crime are located in field offices throughout the country. The IPR Unit and agents work closely with all FBI field offices to combat IP crime. The FBI's IPR Unit encourages victims to report intellectual property crimes through the IPR Center or to any of the FBI's 56 field offices. A list of the FBI field offices is available online at *http://www.fbi.gov/contact-us/field/field-offices*.

❑ **Internet Crime Complaint Center ("IC3").** IC3 is a partnership between the FBI, the National White Collar Crime Center, and the Department of Justice's Bureau of Justice Assistance. IC3 receives, develops, and refers criminal complaints involving a range of cyber crimes including intellectual property crime occurring online. IC3 encourages victims to report complaints involving cyber crime though its website at *http://www.ic3.gov*.

State and Local Investigative Contacts

Federal, state, and local law enforcement agencies and prosecutors all over the country have formed task forces or other working groups to combat computer and intellectual property crime and to promote information sharing between all levels of law enforcement and industry. A state or local task force may be an appropriate contact for cases that do not meet federal criminal thresholds. Examples of these task forces include:

❑ **DOJ-Funded Intellectual Property Enforcement Task Forces.** In the past three years, the Bureau of Justice Assistance, a component of Department of Justice's Office of Justice Programs has awarded over $13 million to 34 state and local law enforcement agencies and three non-profit criminal justice member organizations to support state and local intellectual property law enforcement task forces and local intellectual property training and technical assistance. More information on the grant program is available online at *https://www.bja.gov/ProgramDetails.aspx?Program_ID=64*. To determine whether a task force has been funded in a particular area, see the following link to past grant recipients *https://www.bja.gov/funding.aspx#3*.

❑ **Intellectual Property Theft Enforcement Teams ("IPTET").** ICE-HSI has created 26 IPTETs, in which ICE partners with state, local and tribal law enforcement around the country in informal task forces to enhance coordination of intellectual property investigations. A list of these 26 locations can be found at *http://www.ice.gov/contact/inv/*.

❑ **InfraGard.** The FBI has founded more than 80 chapters of InfraGard – a government and private sector alliance developed to promote the protection of critical information systems – around the country. See *https://www.infragard.net/* for more information about InfraGard generally and to find your local chapter.

❑ **Electronic Crimes Task Forces.** The United States Secret Service has created Electronic Crimes Task Forces in 25 cities. More information on the Electronic Crimes Task Force program and links to the individual task forces can be found at *http://www.secretservice.gov/ectf.shtml*.

Prosecution Contacts

Because of the often complex nature of intellectual property crime and the rapid response required by law enforcement, early engagement of prosecutors often can be helpful. Victims can contact Department of Justice prosecutors in the following ways:

❑ **Computer Hacking and Intellectual Property ("CHIP") Coordinators.** Each of the 93 U.S. Attorneys' Offices throughout the country has at least one Assistant U.S. Attorney who serves as a CHIP coordinator. There are also CHIP units located in 25 districts that have two or more CHIP prosecutors. In total, the Department of Justice has a network of over 260 federal prosecutors who specialize in prosecuting high tech crimes, including intellectual property crimes. The core responsibilities of CHIP prosecutors include (1) prosecuting computer crime and intellectual property offenses; (2) serving as the district's legal counsel on matters relating to those offenses and the collection of electronic or digital evidence; (3) training prosecutors and law enforcement personnel in the region; and (4) conducting public and industry outreach and awareness activities. Victims can contact CHIP prosecutors in their district by calling the local U.S. Attorney's Office and asking for the CHIP prosecutor. A list of U.S. Attorneys' Offices is available online at *http://www.justice.gov/usao/about/offices.html*.

❑ **Computer Crime and Intellectual Property Section ("CCIPS")**. CCIPS is a section within the Department of Justice's Criminal Division. CCIPS has a core team of expert IP prosecutors who prosecute IP crimes and help coordinate multi-district and international IP cases. In addition to prosecution, CCIPS attorneys assist in developing and implementing the Department's overall criminal enforcement strategy to combat intellectual property crime, provide domestic and international training on investigating and prosecuting intellectual property cases, and conduct industry outreach. CCIPS also houses the National CHIP Coordinator to help manage the CHIP Network. In these efforts, CCIPS works closely with the IPTF, U.S. Attorneys' Offices, CHIP coordinators, the IPR Center, and the FBI, among other agencies. More information about CCIPS is available online at *http://www.cybercrime.gov*.

How Can You Assist Law Enforcement?

Prosecutions of intellectual property crime often depend on cooperation between victims and law enforcement. Indeed, without information sharing from intellectual property rights holders, prosecutors can neither discern the trends that suggest the most effective overall enforcement strategies, nor meet the burden of proving an intellectual property offense in a specific case. In addition to the checklist of information that would be helpful to include when reporting a violation, the following seeks to provide guidance concerning the types of ongoing assistance that may be offered by victims of intellectual property crime to law enforcement authorities.

❑ **Identify Stolen Intellectual Property:** Just as in cases involving traditional theft, such as a burglary or shoplifting, victims of intellectual property crime may – and often must – assist law enforcement in the identification of stolen property. Thus, law enforcement may call upon a victim representative or expert to examine items obtained during an investigation to determine their origin or authenticity. In a copyright infringement or counterfeit trademark investigation, for example, an author or software company may be called upon to analyze CDs, DVDs, or other media that appear to be counterfeit, while a victim representative in a theft of trade secret case may be asked to review documents or computer source code. Prosecutors may later seek expert testimony from the victims at trial.

In certain investigations, law enforcement agents also may request a victim's presence during the execution of a search warrant to help the agents identify specific items to be seized. In those circumstances, the victim's activities will be strictly limited to those directed by supervising law enforcement agents.

❑ **Share the Results of Internal Investigations or Civil Lawsuits:** As with any suspected crime, victims may provide law enforcement with information gathered as a result of internal investigations into instances of intellectual property theft. In addition, unless the proceedings or information has been ordered sealed by a court, victims may generally provide law enforcement with any evidence or materials developed in civil intellectual property enforcement actions, including court pleadings, deposition testimony, documents, and written discovery responses.

❑ **Contributions of Funds, Property, or Services:** Donating funds, property, or services to federal law enforcement authorities can raise potential legal and ethical issues that must be addressed on a case-by-case basis. In general, federal law places limitations on contributions to law enforcement authorities.

Checklist for Reporting an Intellectual Property Crime

This checklist serves as a guide for the type of information that would be helpful for a victim or a victim's authorized representative to include when reporting an intellectual property violation to law enforcement. Victims are encouraged to complete the checklist prior to making a report, if possible. Prosecutors and/or investigators may also use the checklist as a framework to gather information from victims. The checklist contains two sections: one intended for use in criminal copyright and trademark cases (including counterfeit trademarks, certification marks or service marks), and the other intended for use in criminal trade secret cases. They can be adapted for use in other intellectual property offenses as well.

Criminal Copyright and Trademark Infringement

✓ Background / Contact Information
✓ Description of the Intellectual Property
✓ Description of the Intellectual Property Crime
✓ Origin and Entry (If Applicable)
✓ Possible Suspects
✓ Internet Involvement
✓ Civil Enforcement Proceedings

Criminal Trade Secret Offenses

✓ Note on Confidentiality
✓ Background / Contact Information
✓ Description of the Trade Secret
✓ Measures Taken to Protect the Physical Trade Secret Location
✓ Confidentiality and Non-Disclosure Agreements
✓ Electronically-Stored Trade Secrets
✓ Document Controls
✓ Employee Controls
✓ Description of the Trade Secret's Misappropriation
✓ Civil Enforcement Proceedings

Criminal Copyright and Trademark Infringement

1. **Background and Contact Information**

    - ❑ Victim's Name:
    - ❑ Primary Address:
    - ❑ Nature of Business:
    - ❑ Primary Contact:
    - ❑ Work Phone:
    - ❑ Mobile Phone:
    - ❑ E-mail:
    - ❑ Fax:

2. **Description of the Intellectual Property**

    - ❑ Describe the copyrighted material or trademark/service mark/certification mark (*e.g.*, title of copyrighted work, identity of logo), including any factors that make its infringement especially problematic (*e.g.*, threats to public health and safety, pre-release piracy).

    - ❑ Is the work or mark registered with the U.S. Copyright Office or on the principal register of the U.S. Patent and Trademark Office?[1] ___ YES ___NO

        If yes, please provide the following:

        - ○ Registration Date:
        - ○ Registration Number:

        If no, state if and when you intend to register:

    - ❑ Do you have a certified copy of the certificate of registration? ___ YES ___NO

---

[1] Registered trademarks can be found through the U.S. Patent & Trademark Office's searchable database at: *http://tess2.uspto.gov/bin/gate.exe?f=tess&state=4010:lmjahh.1.1*

❑ Is the work or mark recorded with U.S. Customs and Border Protection (CBP)?[2]
___ YES ___NO

If yes, please provide the following:

○ Recordation Date:
○ Recordation Number:

❑ What is the approximate retail value of the infringed work, good, or service?

❑ Has the work or mark been the subject of a previous civil or criminal enforcement action? If so, please provide a general description as well as the case name, case number, and name of court.

3. Description of the Intellectual Property Crime

❑ Describe how the theft or counterfeiting was discovered.

❑ Do you have any examination reports of the infringing or counterfeit goods?
___YES ___NO

If yes, please provide those reports to law enforcement. Please also provide a photograph or sample of the goods, if possible.

❑ Describe the type of infringement (*e.g.*, manufacture, reproduction, import, export, distribution).

❑ Describe the scope of the infringing operation, including the following information:

○ Estimated quantity of illegal distribution:
○ Estimated value of illegal distribution:
○ Estimated time period of illegal distribution:
○ Is the illegal distribution national or international? Which states and/or countries?

---

[2] IP rights holders can apply online at https://apps.cbp.gov/e-recordations/ to record their trademarks and copyrights with CBP to protect against the importation of infringing products.

❑ Identify where the infringement or counterfeiting occurred, and describe the location.

4. Origin and Entry (If Applicable)

❑ Identify the country of origin of the infringing item.

❑ Identify the date, location, and mode of entry into the United States.

❑ Identify the names of shippers and Harmonized Tariff Schedule designation and provide any other applicable shipping or customs information.

5. Possible Suspects

❑ Identify the name(s) or location(s) of possible suspects, including the following information:

- ○ Name (Suspect #1):
- ○ Phone number:
- ○ E-mail address:
- ○ Physical address:
- ○ Current employer, if known:
- ○ Any other identifiers:
- ○ Reason for suspicion:
- ○ Name (Suspect #2):
- ○ Phone number:
- ○ E-mail address:
- ○ Physical address:
- ○ Current employer, if known:
- ○ Any other identifiers:
- ○ Reason for suspicion:

6. Internet Involvement

❑ If the distribution of infringing or counterfeit goods involves the Internet, identify the following:

○ How the Internet is involved (*e.g.*, websites, FTP, mail, chat rooms):
○ Relevant Internet address, including any affiliate websites (domain name, URL, IP address, e-mail):
○ Login or password for website:
○ Operators of website, if known:
  ▪ Location of the servers and website host:
  ▪ Country where domain name is registered:
○ Has the right holder sent a cease and desist notice to the website? ___YES ___NO

  If yes, please provide the following:

    ▪ Date of notice:
    ▪ Do you have a copy of the notice? ___ YES ___NO

❑ If you have conducted an internal investigation into the theft or counterfeiting activities, please describe any evidence acquired and submit, if possible, any investigative reports.

7. Civil Enforcement Proceedings

❑ Have you ever received counterfeit goods from the target listed above? ___YES ___NO

❑ If yes, did you place the target on notice that the goods received were counterfeit?

❑ Has a civil enforcement action been filed against the suspects identified above? ___YES ___NO

  If yes, identify the following:

○ Name of court and case number:
○ Date of filing:
○ Names of attorneys:
○ Status of case:

  If no, please state whether a civil action contemplated, what type and when.

❑ Please provide any information concerning the suspected crime not described above that you believe might assist law enforcement.

Trade Secret Offenses

NOTE ON CONFIDENTIALITY

   Federal law provides that courts "shall enter such orders and take such action as may be necessary and appropriate to preserve the confidentiality of trade secrets, consistent with the requirements of the Federal Rules of Criminal and Civil Procedure, the Federal Rules of Evidence, and all other applicable laws." 18 U.S.C. § 1835. Prosecutors utilizing any of the information set forth below will generally request the court to enter an order to preserve the status of the information as a trade secret and prevent its unnecessary and harmful disclosure.

1. Background and Contact Information

- ❑ Victim's Name:
- ❑ Primary Address:
- ❑ Nature of Business:
- ❑ Primary Contact:
- ❑ Work Phone:
- ❑ Mobile Phone:
- ❑ E-mail:
- ❑ Fax:

2. Description of the Trade Secret

- ❑ Generally describe the trade secret (*e.g.*, source code, formula, technology, process, device).

- ❑ Provide an estimated value of the trade secret using one or more of the methods listed below:

Estimated Value	Method
	Cost to develop the trade secret
	Acquisition cost (include date / source of acquisition)
	Fair market value if sold

❑ Provide the name, title and contact information of the person most knowledgeable about the trade secret's valuation:

3. **Measures Taken to Protect the Physical Trade Secret Location**

❑ Describe the company's general security practices concerning entry to and moving within its premises, such as fencing the perimeter of the premises, visitor control systems, using alarming or self-locking doors or security personnel.

❑ Describe any security measures the company has employed to prevent unauthorized viewing or access to the trade secret, such as locked storage facilities or "Authorized Personnel Only" signs at access points.

❑ Describe any protocol the company employs to keep track of employees accessing trade secret material such as sign in/out procedures for access to and return of trade secret materials.

❑ Are employees required to wear identification badges? ___YES ___ NO

❑ Does the company have a written security policy? ___YES ___NO

If yes, please provide the following information:

○ Does the security policy address in any way protocols on handling trade secret information? ___YES ___NO

○ How are employees advised of the security policy?

○ Are employees required to sign a written acknowledgment of the security policy? ___YES ___NO

❑ The name, title, and contact information of the person most knowledgeable about matters relating to the security policy:

❑ How many employees have access to the trade secret?

❑ Was access to the trade secret limited to a "need to know" basis? ___YES ___NO

If yes, describe how "need to know" was maintained in any ways not identified elsewhere (*e.g.*, closed meetings, splitting tasks between employees and/or vendors to restrict knowledge, etc.):

4. Confidentiality and Non-Disclosure Agreements

❑ Does the company enter into confidentiality and non-disclosure agreements with employees and third parties concerning the trade secret? ___YES ___NO

❑ Has the company established and distributed written confidentiality policies to all employees? ___YES ___NO

❑ Does the company have a policy for advising company employees regarding the company's trade secrets? ___YES ___NO

5. Electronically-Stored Trade Secrets

❑ If the trade secret is computer source code or other electronically-stored information, how is access regulated (*e.g.*, are employees given unique user names, passwords, and electronic storage space, and was the information encrypted)?

❑ If the company stores the trade secret on a computer network, is the network protected by a firewall? ___YES ___NO

❑ Is remote access permitted into the computer network? ___YES ___NO

If yes, is a virtual private network utilized? ___YES ___NO

❑ Is the trade secret maintained on a separate computer server? ___YES ___NO

❑ Does the company prohibit employees from using unauthorized computer programs or unapproved peripherals, such as high capacity portable storage devices? ___YES ___NO

❑ Does the company maintain electronic access records such as computer logs? ___YES ___NO

6. Document Controls

❑ If the trade secret consists of documents, were they clearly marked "CONFIDENTIAL" or "PROPRIETARY"? ___YES ___NO

❑ Describe the document control procedures employed by the company, such as limiting access and sign in/out policies.

❑ Was there a written policy concerning document control procedures? ___YES ___NO

If yes, how were employees advised of it?

❑ Provide the name, title, and contact information of the person most knowledgeable about the document control procedures:

7. Employee Controls

❑ Are new employees subject to a background investigation? ___YES ___NO

❑ Does the company conduct regular training for employees concerning steps to safeguard trade secrets?___YES ___NO

❑ Does the company hold "exit interviews" to remind departing employees of their obligation not to disclose trade secrets? ___YES ___NO

8. Description of the Misappropriation of the Trade Secret

❑ Identify the name(s) or location(s) of possible suspects, including the following information:

- ○ Name (Suspect #1):
- ○ Phone number:
- ○ E-mail address:
- ○ Physical address:
- ○ Current employer, if known:
- ○ Any other identifiers:
- ○ Reason for suspicion:
- ○ Name (Suspect #2):
- ○ Phone number:
- ○ E-mail address:
- ○ Physical address:
- ○ Current employer, if known:
- ○ Any other identifiers:
- ○ Reason for suspicion:

❑ Describe how the misappropriation of the trade secret was discovered.

❑ Describe the type(s) of misappropriation (*e.g.*, stealing, copying, drawing, photographing, downloading, uploading, altering, destroying, transmitting, receiving).

❑ Was the trade secret stolen to benefit a third party, such as a competitor or another business? ___YES ___NO

If yes, identify that business and its location.

❑ Do you have any information that the trade secret was stolen to benefit a foreign government or instrumentality of a foreign government? ___YES ___NO

If yes, identify the foreign government or instrumentality and describe that information.

❑ If the suspect is a current or former employee, describe all confidentiality and non-disclosure agreements in effect.

❑ Identify any physical locations associated with the misappropriated trade secret, such as where it may be currently stored or used.

❑ If you have conducted an internal investigation into the misappropriation, please describe any evidence acquired and provide any investigative reports that you can.

9. **Civil Enforcement Proceedings**

❑ Has a civil enforcement action been filed against the suspects identified above?
___YES ___NO

If yes, please provide the following information:

○ Name of court and case number:
○ Date of filing:
○ Names of attorneys:
○ Status of case:

If no, please state whether a civil action contemplated, what type and when.

❑ Please provide any information concerning the suspected crime not described above that you believe might assist law enforcement.